INFLUENCE PEOPLE IN MODERN SOCIETY

Discover How to Read People Like an Open Book and Become a Master of Persuasion & Manipulation. Influence People's Decisions in Your Favor

Table of Content

Introduction 5

Chapter 1 Manipulation as a tool of masters 7
 The secrets of the greatest men 9
 The often overlooked human need to be manipulated 11
 Manipulation is not evil, it's just a tool 13

Chapter 2 Mastering your emotions and reactions 15
 Know YOURSELF (tHIS IS KEY) 15
 Be the master of your emotions 17
 Develop your instincts 20

Chapter 3 Knowledge of emotional reactions and how to read them .. 22
 Knowing your mark 23
 Observing and translating emotional reactions 25
 Learn to take a clue 26
 To react or to obey: The key to always getting it right 27
 Practice makes perfect 28

Chapter 4 Understanding basic body language 29
 Understanding from less than words 31
 The little things are usually most important 35
 Recognizing tells and signs could be an art or science 36
 Recognizing a target 37
 Warning signs 40

Chapter 5 Persuasion: the psychological theories (NEVER FAIL TO CONSIDER THE TARGET) 42
 The psychological perspective 49

Chapter 6 52

Persuasion: The practical 52
Putting the theories into practice 52
Other techniques of persuasion 57
Reverse psychology 62
Remember to always analyze before making your move 63

Chapter 7 Common manipulation techniques 65
Manipulation is not always for the faint hearted 78

Chapter 8 Mastering the art of subtlety-DO NOT BE BLATANT 80
The cautious approach is always best 81
A flimsy ploy is ineffective 82
Never get ahead of yourself 83
Never go all out unless... 83

Chapter 9 Practical uses of manipulation 85
Manipulation in business 85
Manipulation in relationships 87
Manipulating a friend 88
Seductive manipulation 90
How to properly manipulate strangers 90

Chapter 10 Manipulating and Scouting: The Forgotten Connection .. 92
Watching your target is important 93
Establishing trust 94
Planning a strategy of approach 95
Follow only what you see or hear 96

Conclusion 97

Introduction

There is a belief amongst most people that when sequences and situations are created to change the perception and reactions of a person, it is a negative thing. But if we were to look closely, we would observe that this is something that manifests on a daily basis in our lives. we are constantly trying to change how people see us and the things we do. Sometimes we want them to view us in a positive way and other times in a negative way, depending on what we want to achieve at that moment in time. Some people call this manipulation and it is indeed so but manipulation is not necessarily evil as most people would lead you to believe. Many believe it to be associated with only exploitation and deception for personal gain but fail to praise such tactics when they are used positively in eliminating unhealthy habits and behaviors.

To put this in perspective, do you remember the days when your parents had to promise you gifts and extra play time just to get you to complete your homework? That is manipulation in its simplest form but it doesn't match up with what people like to believe of manipulation. They clearly were not manipulating your reasoning for their own benefit, if anything, it was for yours.

People turn to manipulation for a variety of reasons; to advance their own purposes and agendas, to help you attain your own goals and objectives, to gain power or simply because they find it interesting. The last of these reasons is usually the most dangerous because such people are usually oblivious to the damage they can cause or are already causing until they are too far gone in the game. Such people keep manipulating everyone every time without the slightest hint of guilt. Such people are psychopaths.

This audiobook is has not been produced to turn anyone into a psychopath nor is it written to challenge the status quo of manipulation in the world. It is written to show you the ropes at a skill many already utilize. Yes, everyday people manipulate others; in their business environments, in social settings, in friendships and relationships. So, it is high time you sat down and learnt the tricks to an art that all influential people possess.

Chapter 1
Manipulation as a tool of masters

In the world nowadays, a variety of situations necessitates or determines ascribing someone the title of master. But in all of those situations, the master is the one who has most influence on the people around him or her. The power such a master possesses could have initially been attained by skill or reputation but to avoid losing it over time, the master has to be adept at retaining his or her influence. Such a person is usually held in high regard, regardless of status or wealth and vary rarely do these people attain such a status by being themselves or by being ordinary. Being so might make people to like and admire you but true respect and power over others must be gotten by other means. This is where manipulation comes in.

Manipulation goes hand in hand with power. Wherever you can sense the effect of manipulation, there is bound to be an imbalance of power. The power in such societies is usually concentrated in the hands of a few who could be referred to as masters over others. These people are well versed at making people think along the same lines as them, making people act along the same lines as them, making people follow them unconditionally and generally being able to influence the thoughts and opinions of those around them effectively.

If you were to look back in history at some of the most influential people, one of the things you would observe is that the ideas they advocated were not necessarily moral or even right at all. Their beliefs were not necessarily righteous or ethical, but whenever they needed it, people and followers flocked to their sides, ready to follow them to the end and ready to defend the ideas they had been taught to believe and defend. From terrorist leaders to controversial politicians and men of power who regardless of the revulsion their ideas seemed to generate still seemed to be gaining more power. Why was this so? Because they knew how to influence and control people. It didn't matter what they said but provided they could make people think how they wanted them to and act how they wanted them to, they were never at risk of being powerless. Their power didn't originate from a sense of righteousness or correctness but from the sense of followership they were able to instill in people.

It is this sense of followership and loyalty that you should aim to achieve through manipulation. Manipulation is not just your key to power, it is your key to success because with power comes the ability to thrive off people in any environment. This ability is inherent in all successful people. Whether you are an entrepreneur or someone with a daily job, as long as people are involved, the knowledge of people and how to influence them is necessary for your success.

Some people have those once in a lifetime ideas or a revolutionary approach to solving a problem but without the knowledge of how to thrive on the backs of others, they would never be able to fully consolidate on what they have. The ability to manipulate people is yours to use as you wish; you could use it in your search for personal happiness or in your quest for wealth and affluence, whichever one is your choice. This book, however, has only one aim; helping you become a master in whatever you chose to be or do.

The secrets of the greatest men

Manipulation and deception are one of the numerous skills possessed by the greatest and most powerful men to have roamed this earth. Not all men are Gandhi and if the history books were properly scoured and its annals scrutinized, many of the men who have exerted the most influence on the world would be shown to be manipulators who merely hid their more negatively perceived talents in a shroud of piety, idealism and oratory.

This is not to say that these men were evil or bad, they just understood the need to do what was necessary when necessary and if this involved tweaking the emotions and thoughts of people to generate reactions that were favorable to their causes, so be it.

And so, the truth behind many of the world's greatest men and leaders is not divine intervention or an alignment of the stars but rather a lack of the emotional restrictions that plague the ordinary man. Many of these men from Caesar to Napoleon weren't evil or psychopathic but had a goal and a vision of the world that couldn't be achieved by simply following the rules and hoping that every other person saw things the same way they did. No, great men do not wait, they act.

Not to limit this to only men, we have had some pretty powerful women in the past who understood that to wield real power was not a matter of honesty or being a good wife but rather how to get people to do what you want when you want it. That is the essence of manipulation, to get people so dependent and so in awe of you that you could easily influence their principles and guide their actions in the direction you believe it ought to be going in. Take for instance, the sexual manipulation of both Caesar and Mark Anthony by Cleopatra in a bid to protect her interests and titles. It is mostly overlooked but that has in no way detracted from her brilliant manipulation of two very powerful men.

What I am trying to say here is that many of the events that have shaped the world politically, industrially, even religiously are so mired in manipulation, it's hard to dismiss its usefulness in both the old days and the modern world. It is used as a business tactic, as a means of motivation or as an aid to persuasion in almost any facet of life.

In the modern world, manipulation is synonymous with politics and is widely thought to be used only by politicians, business executives and the likes but if you look closely, you would see that we all practice a form of manipulation. In fact, any setting in which there seems to be an imbalance of power probably contains an element of manipulation and since this imbalance in power is a staple of the realistic world, it could be said that manipulation is rife in the world and in our everyday life. There is manipulation in our daily interactions, in our personal relationships, our business relationships and even religious interactions. Consider the clergy who spends a large chunk of his sermon emphasizing on punishment of sin and the travails of hell, he might be speaking the truth but his words are meant to impart fear in you and it is that fear which he counts on to make the difference in your approach to life. That is a classic case of emotional manipulation using fear. The cleric does not mean to do this but deep down he realizes that this is the most effective way of knocking into people the need for his or her God. He does not mean to manipulate you but he does it nonetheless. That is what manipulation is. You might truly respect the autonomy of a person but when you feel you need to influence them, you could unknowingly find yourself trying to take advantage of their emotions and this means you are manipulating them. You do not have to be evil, you simply need to recognize the necessity for a line of action and possess the strength of mind to do what needs to be done.

Over the course of this audio book, you would learn how to wield similar power over people, how to make yourself indispensable and how to make yourself capable of greatness.

The often overlooked human need to be manipulated

As humans we have all been blessed with autonomy, the right to make our own decisions and live by them and any threat to such autonomy generally has us on guard. That is the reason why when faced with anything, law or person we believe aims to rip this independence from us, we fight back with or without violence. Take into consideration the numerous uprisings in history as proof of this. The people who led the French and English revolutions did not possess more power than the monarchs in power but when they felt their needs being thrown out the door and their independence being preyed upon, they fought back and they fought hard.

Our history when it comes to defending our independence is quite rich, from the early advocates of our modern religions facing up to the idol worshippers in their day to the women throughout history who have fought for equal rights. They might not have realized what they were doing but they were exercising an innate human need to be free. But just as the need to be free exists, so does the need to be controlled or the need for order.

This need to be controlled is the reason why humans needed monarchs and governments to rule and govern their daily life. Because if left to live life freely and unchecked, we would have been consumed by chaos. But as our population grew and we expanded to cover more territory, so did the influence of such monarchs and governments, the controlling forces, on our life wear thin, eventually becoming insignificant. Though this is on a much grander scale and might, it is a larger manifestation of our need to sometimes be guided by others. Thus, it is apt to say that every one of us needs guidance.

The guidance might be spiritual, academic or psychological but if we were to trace the source of our knowledge, we would find that it must have originated from a person or book and very rarely is it completely original. To better understand this, consider how you always feel the need to try and impart the knowledge you have unto others either by holding lectures or by giving advice. This need to guide one another is how we humans have passed our knowledge over millenniums.

It is because of this inherent need for guidance, knowledge and control that we are susceptible to manipulation. I am not saying that anybody deserves to be manipulated but that everybody can be manipulated. And since whatever is possible is always done, the possibility of being manipulated means that some of us, or rather, many of us are bound to fall victim to people whose goal is to manipulate us. It is the way of the world, the only difference between you and the next person is how good you are at it and how you want to use your influence and skill.

Manipulation is not evil, it's just a tool

It is widely believed that manipulation is evil, I neither support nor assent to this belief. Manipulation is the use of any sort of influence, be it physical, emotional or financial, over a person, group or situation to generate a desired outcome. The outcome is most likely one which favors you and your goals but does not necessarily need to be detrimental to other people involved. On another note, the belief of manipulation being negative usually assumes that this goal you want to achieve is not in sync with that of your mark or target. But, what if it does? Won't it then be more apt to classify your manipulation as a means of motivation or, at the very least, as a positive influence? Consider this:

You have a boss who is hell bent on following a particular line of action as regards a new business deal yet facts and your gut tell you that his approach or decision is a wrong one. But he refuses to listen to the opinions of anyone, probably because his stance is as a result of a very old sentiment or bias. In this case, every straightforward and honest approach has failed. Wouldn't it be better to manipulate and tweak his emotions just a little bit and save his job and the company's balance sheet from recording a loss?

In such a case, your manipulation of your boss is still considered immoral but on the general balance of events, it is the right course of action if all means of rational persuasion have been exhausted. From a conventional point of view, the idea of one person manipulating another is considered a criticism of the manipulator's behavior, but is manipulation always immoral? The above example doesn't seem immoral. When looked at on a grander scale, we would most likely agree that manipulation is rife in our everyday life but the only times it is actually classified as evil or bad is when it leads to harm, be it emotional or psychological, of the target. Sure, manipulation can expose vulnerabilities that otherwise might have remained hidden. Yes, manipulation could lead to oppression of people but it could also be the only way to achieve a truly noble goal. Consider this next example.

Assuming you are a security officer who was unlucky enough to be on duty on the day a terrorist was captured and you have credible intel that the terrorist is slated to carry out an attack on that very day or maybe during the week. You have tried every possible method of rational reasoning from trying to tap into his or her empathy to offering deals but the terrorist has refused to budge and the only way to extract the information without resorting to violence is to employ manipulation as a tool. Is this considered immoral or is the immorality simply justified simply because you get to save many lives?

Depending on your answer to the above question, the knowledge shared in this book might one day be beneficial to you. If you possess a hardline view on the perception of manipulation and are of the opinion that it can never be used for a positive goal, the knowledge of this book is of no practical use to you and you are better served stopping here and picking a book that is more acceptable and is less likely to offend your sensibilities.

Chapter 2
Mastering your emotions and reactions

Manipulation is a game of emotions, knowing how to read them, how to tweak them, how to play them, erase them, create them and react to them. Every manipulative move should be aimed at exposing the emotional core of your mark or target because that is the only way to owning their actions and decisions. But for you to adequately and efficiently effect your desired change in the individual or group of relevance, you have to have an understanding of yourself and your emotions. To put it cleanly, you have to know yourself more than any other person because only then can you make a move at controlling others.

Know YOURSELF (tHIS IS KEY)

Knowing yourself is key if not the most important ingredient to possess before you embark on the road to mastering people. This is because, to avoid overreaching or underestimating yourself, you have to possess an understanding of your abilities, a keen sense as to where your strengths end and where your weaknesses begin. Only with this knowledge can you decipher the direction in which you should be leading your mark and the approach you should be taking to do so.

Such in depth knowledge of oneself would require a level of truthfulness in accepting one's limitations and a further level of self-discipline to avoid crossing those limits. The idea behind getting under your target's defenses would vary depending on the target but would require you to either play up your weaknesses while emphasizing your strengths or play up your strengths while emphasizing your weaknesses. Both require you to be alert.

As important as understanding your limits is, it would be nothing without an understanding of your emotions and that would be incomplete without the ability to recognize your emotional markers. These markers are what people see regardless of what goes on in your head and thus, are more likely to influence their thoughts. This knowledge is not achieved by simply making a resolution but by logically analyzing your every move in a bid to pinpoint how your internal emotions manifest as external actions. This might seem complex but it is actually quite easy. It just involves thinking about your reactions and emotion as two separate entities then following them through step by step to the end and figuring out how one influences the other. Let me give you a hypothetical situation.

A friend of yours who is usually quiet and reserved walks up to you one day and shoves you in the back in a moment of excitement. It was a playful shove but you not realizing it were this particular friend turns back and are about to express your anger before you notice him and check yourself. He sees this and wonders why you would react in such a way and in a playful manner shoves you again. This time however, you don't check yourself but instead launch into a tirade.

At the time he hit you the first time, let's assume you were in a rather normal state, not particularly angry or happy. After the first hit, you got angry but controlled yourself. While this control is necessary to possess for the skill you are learning, the important part of your analysis should be what gave your anger away since you had not actually reacted. You have to know if it was a clenched fist by your side, a hardened facial expression, a twitching eye or whatever because controlling the reaction is only half the lesson, you have to behave outwardly like the thought of a reaction never even crossed your mind. This is the kind of logical breakdown you must grow adept at performing on yourself and your actions. You must abandon the ordinary man's habits of reacting impulsively and start reacting logically. Next, you have to consider your loss of control on the succeeding incident. Such a reaction could point to the shove itself being an act that ticks you off, an underlying problem or problems with the aforementioned friend or even your limit in such situations. Whichever one it is, you need to get a handle on it and eliminate all emotions from your reactions unless when you feel it has to be released.

Be the master of your emotions

Other than your strengths and weaknesses, another key area of your life and being to pay attention to is your emotions. Most people underestimate the need for a control over their emotions and that is the major reason they have little control over the emotions of others. I am not advising for you to remain meek regardless of the provocation or for you to flare up at the slightest sign of resistance. No, what I am saying is that you have to be able to control whatever reaction is necessary in the moment, to bring it out at a moment's notice and to lock it back up when it has served its purpose. You need to recognize your emotional triggers and work at dulling their effect. Failing at such an important facet of your person could lead you to unwillingly push a target too far or to allow a target run wild and free for too long. Meanwhile, mastering the control of your emotion in this way would give the double advantage of reducing the ability people possess to rile you up or manipulate you while also granting you complete autonomy over your own reactions.

As I implied earlier, different targets require different approaches and different treatments and for this reason different emotions would elicit different effects on them. Where anger might cause one to be subservient, it might cause another to be more belligerent. This is the major reason you have to master not just the ability to act and create emotional reactions but also the ability to suppress your more natural emotional reactions as these said reactions can interfere with the image you are trying to portray.

Your control on your emotions is one of the major tools by which you control the perception people have of you and when it comes to manipulating people, it is key that you control their perception of you because only then would you control how they will treat you. It is important for you to remember that the initial way by which people judge another's character is through his or her behavior and emotional disposition and as such, control over both would grant onto you the power to control people's perception of you.

From another angle, your emotional disposition towards issues and events is usually a cornerstone of your reputation, at least in the minds of most people. This is a weakness in people. They assume that emotions are almost unchangeable thereby nullifying the possibility in their minds that one is capable of manipulating his or her emotions to deceive them. They believe that your reaction to a situation would always stay constant unless another effect is in play. The trick is introducing another reaction/emotion that contradicts your normal in a bid to gain their attention while lowering their defenses to deal with your perceived soft spot.

Because of this nullification, this is a belief you must always be out to take advantage of. The warning behind this is that before attempting to cash in on this mistake, you have to have fine-tuned your ability to act out scenarios and create emotions. If you are not well versed at this, a smart target might figure out your play before you are even started.

Furthermore, when utilizing this weakness, the emotion being introduced should be as evanescent as possible so as not to confuse the target. What I mean is that, with such a tactic, the effect you are going for is the **"oh, that is so unlike him"** effect and not the **"oh, he has changed so much from the time we met"** effect. This means that the emotion to be introduced should be temporary and fleeting, only surfacing for a brief period of time. Most times, the tactic is effective for a particular emotion only once or twice and should never be attempted consecutively using the same emotion. Here is an illustration of this particular trick.

The target is a female and you have gone through the basics with her, establishing a character and manufacturing reactions for every predictable action of hers. In your bid to seduce her, you have gotten to first base, first kiss and now you are looking to score a big finish and leave. But she's been very coy and defensive about sex and you haven't been able to lower her defenses on the issue. One day an issue comes up between you guys and ordinarily you would have let it slide with a smile but instead you flare up for a bit and take to keeping to yourself. She avoids bringing up the issue for a while but later comes in for the conversation.

The major point here is the change from your regular emotional reaction to a more aggressive one. This would prompt her to believe that you might have lost a little bit of emotional control and seeing as such instability is a constant source of discussion in relationships, your current countenance would require her to have a conversation with you. Bear in mind that the conversation is not for you to petulantly complain about her not having sex with you but rather for you to make her feel she is in a position of power to broker peace while considering you to be the victim. You are not to make things overly hard or easy for her. Your time to act would come after you have settled the quarrel. It would be right for you to initiate a make out session rather than ask her to have sex. This moment in which she has lowered her defenses to accommodate your emotional issues is when you make your move and if you have played your cards right up to that moment, you are about to get that score you have been hoping for. From then onwards, it is up to you to proceed as you wish but with smarts of course. Do not forget, overusing this tactic increases the possibility of exposing your game to your target.

Develop your instincts

Instincts are natural; they are either borne from experience or you are born with them. It is that voice in your head that speaks to you when you are in a fix and need a quick solution to your problem. It is the one that guides most of your impulsive reactions. I bet you used to doubt your impulses could change but trust me they can. Many people believe impulses can only be controlled but that is for someone who still wants to possess impulses. Real masters of emotions do not just control their impulses, they eliminate them.

Only when those impulses are absent do the instincts you have trained yourself in start to kick in.

Our instincts are a product of our deeper nature, our deeper understanding and our environment. They usually mirror the things we have learnt and experienced. When we act on our instincts, were basically surrendering to our past experiences and innermost directions. These directions can be changed but not easily. To truly develop your instincts is not a matter of turning pages or staring at a screen and absorbing words but rather putting your skills to the test in real life and facing failure because only with these can you correct the folly of past experiences and create new directions. You have to put your newly learned tactics to work, feel them out, recognize how to make them click for you and depending on what you succeed or fail at, your mind will automatically store all of these experiences as either positive results inducing actions or negative results inducing actions. It is based on the presence of this more advanced knowledge that your instincts become sharper and more trustworthy because you stop making decisions steeped in theoretical propaganda and start making experienced decisions.

Instincts are necessary in understanding people and situations because only when you know what to look out for can you correctly react but in instances when the mark is still more of a stranger, you have to rely on your instincts and experiences to guess what type of person you are dealing with in terms of temperament, likes, dislikes, potential tells and the likes. Without the necessary sharp instincts, these would be quite difficult if not impossible.

Chapter 3
Knowledge of emotional reactions and how to read them

Reading people is arguably the most vital tool to a successful manipulation. This might be an art to some or a science to others depending on if they are naturally talented at it or if it is a completely acquired skill. Don't get me wrong, I do not mean to say that some are born with the ability to read people. What I mean is that it comes easier to some people with time than others.

Reading people and their emotions is a historically difficult task and yet without it, attempting a manipulation is akin to a blind man climbing a mountain. Many believe it to be about making snap decisions based on how people look and jumping to conclusions before you have even shared a word but in truth, it is way more than that. Before we jump into this, I should warn you that psychologists have confirmed that there is no foolproof way to read or decipher people and I would like to personally add that many of the methods you might learn might seem contradictory. Having said this, it is up to you to engage your wits and let your instincts guide you.

A key facet of reading people is their emotional disposition towards various situations. To really understand them through this means, you need to have watched them react to a few situations so as to give you a feel as to how they might react in similar and contrasting settings. However, emotions are notoriously difficult to decipher and many amateurs make the mistake of translating signs and gestures into singular meanings. This is wrong because a sign could denote multiple possible emotions.

It is due to this possibility that signs and gestures should not be treated or read as individual entities but rather should be taken contextually, while also putting into consideration other facts available to you. The last ingredient that is needed to make the result of a reading as close to reality as possible is a sharp instinct. I have spoken about developing this in chapter 2 and will refrain from discussing further but in my opinion, it is the most important tool for reading people.

Knowing your mark

The first step to reading a mark or target is to abandon all of your previous projections and prejudices about people. These prejudices could be racial, ethnic etc. but they should all be thrown out because without a clean slate on which to present your facts, you risk destroying your readings with bias and sentiments. As a manipulator, your main goal in reading people, especially strangers, is not to spot deceit but to spot openings which could be used to forge connections or to discover character traits that could be used to your advantage. I would advise that when initially attempting manipulations, you pick targets that are more insecure, lonely or are possessing of low self-esteem. This is usually obvious from their need to defend themselves regularly, an eagerness to join or participate in a conversation, shyness, tendency to back down from confrontations and similar behaviors.

A general way to get people to initially lower their defenses with you is to act charming. Do not act all weird and slimy with them but adopt a natural witty charm, the kind reserved for your principal or favorite high school teacher back in the day. This is especially effective with shy or insecure targets, people who would welcome compliments and are more likely to warm to jokes and strangers faster.

Another way is to break down the trust barrier by offering a little of yourself and your secrets first. This part of you doesn't necessarily have to be true but it must be believable. Once the primary connection is formed however, it is time to begin information gathering. If your mark is talkative, you are in luck. Simply keep quiet and let the prattle run. There is bound to be at least a tidbit of information scattered in between. However, if the target is more reserved or quieter, a little bit of skillful prodding is needed to tap into the right vibe and once you get it, be sure to keep the buzz going for as long as possible.

Other than information garnered from conversation, you can also proceed to watch the crowd he/she hangs out with, her favorite drinks, favorite color and hobbies. This might seem very banal but knowledge of them could give you an in with the mark and that's all that is needed to improve your status in their lives. Once you have established the right relationship, the next step is to hunt for the more private bits of information, the ones most likely to push the buttons you need pushed.

Observing and translating emotional reactions

To properly observe a person's reactions and understand the logic or motive behind them, you have to take an objective perspective of the person's actions, devoid of any connections whatsoever. To do this you first have to establish the nature of the events or situations causing such a reaction to check for its conventionality because since most people tend to react conventionally to certain things, the abnormalities and oddities are the ones to look out for. Next, you analyze the markers of these reactions in the person so that if such a reaction were to occur for another stimulus, it would be clear what such a person is feeling. Some emotions may possess the same marker and would therefore require secondary markers or experience with the target to tell them apart.

The need for marking the emotional reaction of the target as well as its causes is to be well placed to use the emotions to your advantage. Also knowing the tells would expose to you the presence of a particular emotion, allowing you to adapt to the mood and needs of the person thus keeping yourself relevant while making them believe that you care. This might probably only be necessary at the beginning of the association as the person is more likely to show more subservience or dependence as the manipulations grows deeper.

Deciphering and translating the emotions of a person might seem tricky at first but usually gets easier with time. For instance, staying with a new cousin, family relative or roommate might be difficult at first but as you start to warm up to them and learn about their eccentricities, what makes them tick and what kills their buzz, their secrets begin to up to you one at a time. It's the same way with targets of manipulations; you need to invest time in understanding and learning their reactions and what they mean so as to avoid pushing the wrong buttons at the wrong times.

Learn to take a clue

Very rarely, you might encounter an oddity that more or less does not conform to the reading you have arrived at on a particular person, do not fret and do not react too swiftly. It is better to ignore it outwardly while watching for signs of repetition. The smart play would be to analyze it, try to understand what brought about the anomaly and if it is likely to happen again. This is necessary because manipulation is about control of not only the target but of everything affecting the target that can be controlled. Those that cannot be controlled should be predicted and skillfully avoided to prevent any surprises from occurring.

Take for example, you have cultivated a manipulative relationship with a young lady or man who is quite reserved and is more prone to long periods of silence. Then on a night out together, the target completely flips script and goes all wild partygoer on you, do not react hastily. It could be as a result of something or someone in their life that you are not familiar with and a hasty reaction against a previously entrenched stimulus could be rather counterproductive. Instead, it would be advisable for you go along with the flow and later question their behavior. This would enable you to gain the knowledge you want without relinquishing control of the situation.

This is the idea behind taking a clue. You have to be ready to adapt and shift your position to better understand a situation.

To react or to obey: The key to always getting it right

This is one of my favorite rules because it requires patient thinking and smart decision making. The translation is rather simple. To react is to adopt an active approach while to obey is to do otherwise. The rule applies to you, the manipulator, and the target. It is simply used to stop impulsive action. The question is quite straightforward, do you react to a situation or let things slide?

This question is one you should never fail to ask yourself before putting another ploy in motion. It would be reckless of you if you were to move too fast and sloppy of you if you were to move too slowly. That is where the question comes in. It challenges you to consider your status and decide if any further action is necessary. Failure to make the right choice often ends in regret.

An alternative question, mostly used at the beginning of a manipulation to better gauge the chances of success of the ploy, is to ask yourself how smart your target truly is. This might seem ordinary but for you to succeed you have to have complete faith in your own abilities while steering clear of overconfidence and most times a good perception of the targets own intellect is the perfect constraint.

As effective as this rule could be, there is no trick or shortcut to knowing the answer to the question. To react or to obey could only be answered by you. You are to put every piece of information you possess on the target into play and then consult your gut and instincts on whether one or the other is the right choice. You would probably stumble a few times during the learning process but you could also be a natural, getting it right every single time. Whichever it is, remember to always learn from your experiences because only through our experiences are we ever truly equipped to deal with the future.

Practice makes perfect

As previously stated, manipulation has to be worked at constantly to attain the level at which success becomes the norm. Practice and constant use of the skills you learn would sharpen your skills as regards people and how they should be dealt with. All the advice in this book are merely words on a piece of paper or an audio recording without your own ability to bring them to life. Everyone is different and as such, different methods work for them. This applies to you as much as it applies to your target. You have to be able to bring the ideas in this book in a way that suits your character and approach and there is no better way to learn to do this than by practicing.

Manipulation is a game that deals with emotions and constant practice is perfect to boost your instincts as well as your confidence. Stick to these rules and warning and it's only a matter of time before you become a master manipulator. Just like in every other field, without sharp instincts, you are ordinary, without experience you carry a large chance of failure, without confidence you can do nothing. Practice is important if you are to achieve all three and rise above being ordinary.

Chapter 4
Understanding basic body language

When two people meet each other, it doesn't matter whether they are old friends or new acquaintances, they could even be strangers, but they communicate through not only words but gestures. These gestures tend to betray our mental state and express how we are feeling. For instance, if were feeling bad and irritable, we give off defensive signals and when we are feeling happy, we tend to be more relaxed and friendlier.

These gestures and signals relay our mood to the person or persons around us and affects what they think and how they relate with us at that moment in time. This ability to read basic and common gestures is rather inherent in every one but as a result of practice and experience some people are more adept at it than others. For example, women are generally more perceptive to gestures than men, probably due to the fact that they might have had lots of practice dealing with their kids or those of others.

Many common gestures such as crying, laughing and frowning denote the same emotional and mental state in most people with very little exceptions. However, your emphasis on body language and gestures as a manipulator should go beyond the study of the more common gestures if you hope to become a master. It should at least encompass the knowledge of basic body language for you to truly appreciate its effect on your everyday choices and decisions. You should also be able to notice and translate a wide range of uncommon expressions.

Gestures and signals could mean many things in different places, so it would be wise to observe the general trends around wherever you stay and ask questions when necessary before jumping to needless conclusions. Furthermore, the frequencies with which these gestures occur vary with a variety of factors. One of these is age. It has been proven that the older people get the lesser the gestures they use in communicating their opinions. Another factor is wealth or social class. It has also been noticed that people higher up the social chain in a particular environment use fewer gestures than those below them. These are all generalizations and exceptions to such are bound to occur. For example, people who are very excited tend to gesticulate more and those who are bored, take on a more reserved demeanor. Thus, a bored teenager could probably use less gestures and body movement in expressing him or herself than an excited septuagenarian. In such a case, the age generalization would have failed.

Well, other than these generalizations, it is important to pay attention to the particular gestures of each person while also monitoring their verbal output. Look for contradictions that give the person away as regards whether they are lying or hiding something and make your next steps based on these deductions. The most effective way of catching lying in a person is to watch out for gestures that betray their true intention. Such gestures or behaviors are usually out of place or out of sync with the message they are delivering or trying to deliver.

Understanding from less than words

The ability to tell as much as possible about a person without engaging in conversations is one that would help you well, especially when it comes to securing and developing a new target. When I say developing a target, I mean the first few conversations and meetings you have in which you try to determine the attitude and emotional disposition of the person towards key issues so as to better mold the character you would assume around them.

This understanding of a person could aid your quest in many ways. It could portray you as someone who is perceptive and sensitive to their need and this is a good way of establishing trust within the target. It could also be useful in predicting the actions of a person so as to better react to them. This reaction could be in many forms varying from a modified approach to a subject to a complete avoidance of another. It is, in summary, a good way to avoid falling afoul of a person before you have been able to achieve what you initially set out to achieve.

Many signs could actually mean more than one thing and should not be taken as a complete truth but rather as a possible truth. What this means is that, all possible translations should be considered before you jump to any final conclusions. This is due to the fact that more than one factor could be in play and probably the telling factor causing a particular reaction is not even from us but from another person or situation entirely. Such consideration should apply to both positive and negative reactions because we, as humans, tend to apply this to only the negatives while imagining all positive reactions to be of our own making. I am going to consider the reactions we should or could expect in a first meeting because I assume that after the first meeting, your status or likely status should be established already. Let us begin with reactions to expect in a first meeting.

1. **Acceptance and rejection:** Being able to perceive whether someone is digging you or accepting your approach is quite important as it tells you a lot about the success of your current approach on the person and whether or not you may need to change it. Though it is very difficult to know if your message is getting through, little gestures such as moving closer and interrupting every now and then to put in a point should bolster your confidence that your presence is at least not unwanted. In fact, if you really want to judge whether or not your company is pleasing to the person, it would be more apt to look for the signals of rejection rather than those of acceptance. You should look for signs such as how regularly the person offers an opinion during a conversation, how frequently and how sincerely the person smiles or laughs at your jokes, whether the person retreats whenever you move closer and how long the person spends in a side conversation with another friend before returning to you and whether or not they apologize.

The regularity with which the person offers opinions show how much the person is concentrating on your words and this in turn denotes if and how interesting your company is. If the person speaks only a little, it could mean that the person doesn't like you or is bored. Anyhow, if walking away is not an option, you could resort to asking a question and using the persons answer to change the topic. Watch out for changes in their reactions to gauge their concentration.

Someone who laughs frequently and sincerely at your jokes is definitely enjoying the conversation and is less likely to leave soon. However, someone who just stares at you after a joke or gives a weak smile is probably not impressed by you or your wit. But before jumping to conclusions, the blank stare could also be as a result of a lack of understanding on their part.

If after a few moments of a conversation, you attempt to lean in to emphasize a point and the target (mostly females in this case) retreats, taking a step or two back, it could mean that she doesn't like you, she still considers you a stranger, she is surprised or she simply isn't feeling the conversation as much as you thought. it might even be due to mouth odor. The trick with dealing with this is to stay calm and pretend not to notice this. Continue with the conversation as naturally as possible and after a few minutes, attempt to lean in again. If she retreats again, it is probably due to one of the first two possible reasons or the mouth odor.

During conversations with a person, it is quite common for side conversations with a passing friend to occur. The duration of this side conversation could however be of significance when it comes to determining how they view you. If the side conversation goes on for so long that you look and feel like you are standing all alone and yet the person with whom you were conversing hasn't offered an apology, the meaning is quite bad. But if the person constantly cuts short the side conversation to apologize to you an even takes the hard decision of cutting short and postponing such a conversation, it means your presence is at least appreciated and not unwanted. If the former was actually the case, it could be due to the fact that the target considers your presence to be boring, and the side conversation to be a needed reprieve. If this is so walk away and do not return, unless the target approaches you. Save your dignity.

2. Happiness: Someone who immediately warms up to you in a first meeting or conversation and is happy to have your company would most likely participate in the conversation, not just butting in to express opinions but also to tell stories and crack jokes. Such a person is also likely to laugh a lot and may even attempt to introduce you to a few more people if you are a stranger at whatever place you are meeting. It is also possible that the person is intoxicated and their overly positive reaction is due to whatever intoxicant they might have ingested. The best way to deal with this is to go on with the flow and probably try getting their contact information for a future meeting but keeping whatever conclusions you may have had aside for when such a meeting comes. A distant possibility is that they are utilizing your company to achieve a goal of their own, say, making someone jealous. I classified this as a distant possibility because it rarely happens but I still felt the need to mention it so as to stress the need for you to always consider all options and to always stay aware of everything going on around you and your target.

3. Distaste or dislike: This is different from rejection in that the person in this case would probably not even be polite enough to answer you properly. It is rather easy to spot and could include signs like a frown, lack of eye contact and short or monosyllabic answers. If this happens to you, do not inquire as to what might be wrong or what you might have done wrong. Instead, say your goodbyes and walk away. If you are to approach such a person again, be sure to have a friend of theirs there to introduce you first. This could make all the difference.

The possible scenarios are endless but these are the most popular reactions you could come up against. The reason for outlining these situations and how to deal with them is to enable you use the knowledge of basic body language and how to properly react to them to better make a first conversation or meeting as fruitful as possible. If dealing with failure and rejection is not a strong point of yours, it might be better to watch from a distance how such a person relates with others and judge using these same skills, how to approach such a person or if he or she is worth the stress.

The little things are usually most important

We have touched on some of the more elaborate and obvious gestures and the little ones are up next. These are called little because they are mostly imperceptible and are done very quickly. They are those things one is likely to miss or overlook such as a quick lick of the lip, a glance at a wristwatch or clock, a glance at another person or even running a hand through their hair. These things are likely to possess meanings that are particular to different people and as such, the same meaning might not apply to different people. These types of reactions should not be studied and translated as individual events or reaction but instead as a part of a larger one.

To adequately guess the meaning to this sort of reactions, you need to consider other gestures that might have come immediately before it, what the target was saying at the moment of the reaction and any possible contradictions between the two. The truth is such reactions rarely occur only once. Most times they are conditioned reflexes in the person to help them deal with something they are otherwise uncomfortable with. It is equally as rare for anyone to recognize any of these reactions not to talk of translating it without spending a tremendous amount of time with the person. For this reason, such reactions are psychological gold and should be cherished.

These inherent reactions are what we call tells.

Recognizing tells and signs could be an art or science

The ability to instantly recognize a tell or sign in a person when you see one could be an in born or a developed attribute. one could simply spend a few weeks with people and be able to reveal three or four tells that point to how the target is really feeling while other spend years and still struggle to recognize one. This is no reason to worry because while the ability to notice and translate tells makes manipulation easier, the absence of such a skill doesn't make it impossible. Having said this, it should be noted that recognizing such tells can be learnt so, if you lack the natural knack for seeing them, you can still manipulate your target but knowing how to recognize some would definitely be advantageous.

Some tells could be the tendency for a person to run his or her hands through the hair, crossing of the fingers, rapid blinking, twitching of the eye, rapping the knuckles on a surface and many others. These seem like actions that denote rather obvious emotions but most tells are. The major issue with a tell is that these obvious actions do not actually follow an easily perceivable emotion and are usually done so quickly, they could be mistaken for necessary. Thus, to notice them, one must be observant and to translate them, you might have a good grasp of whatever situation them might have occurred under. Isolating the situation and breaking it down into a list of potential stimuli could help in narrowing down the possible meanings.

Recognizing a target

One of the most important things for being a good manipulator is the ability to notice the right people, the ability to pick the right targets. Well, sorry, there are no right targets. The truth is that everyone can be manipulated by a master but it takes a lot of practice to become a master and as such, for beginners like you, picking the easy or more susceptible targets is the smarter move.

Generally speaking, the easiest people to manipulate are usually those with low self-esteem, low self-confidence or other form of insecurities. These traits usually manifest in numerous forms and it is these forms you have to be trained to notice.

- **Naivety:** This is a very popular draw for manipulation because the victim is almost never aware that he or she possesses such a trait and this limits the possibility that they will eventually discover you. It could be noticed clearly in people who always strive to see the best in others. Such a person even when confronted with the idea and even evidence of manipulation is likely to still believe everything is a coincidence and should have another explanation. This is definitely one you should look out for.

- **Emotional dependence:** People who exhibit this trait are almost always in relationships and such relationships are almost always ending. Why is this? Because their happiness depends on the happiness of others and due to this, they could be considered needy. But their neediness is to your advantage. These sorts of people would do anything to keep you happy, even if it goes against their best interests and the best thing is, they'd do it quite willingly. This would mean little effort from you and an almost servile target. The only caveat to this type of person is that, they are mostly always the jealous types. Be careful.

- **Low self-confidence:** If you have ever met someone with low self-confidence, you'd agree with me that they are always seeking validation of their actions and decisions and these tend to expose them to manipulation. As a manipulator, your power over this class of people lies in your approval and the way you use it. Withholding such an approval makes them eager, to please and giving the approval makes them happy, relaxed and ripe for the taking.

- **Pseudo-manipulators:** Have you ever met people who like to feel like they are the smartest and the most powerful in the room? If yes, this is their class. People like this usually feel like they can prey on others and are good manipulators but in truth are nothing but failures. They are very hard to find but if you ever meet a person who acts out manipulative tendencies but possesses no real influence on people, you have your mark. The way to handle such people is to play the victim or subordinate and strive to avoid doing their wishes while making sure they do yours. This might involve a whole lot of acting and a few concessions at the beginning but would definitely be worth the hassle at the end. These people are mostly narcissists and are easy to pick out using this very trait.

- **Lack of assertiveness:** These kinds of people do not have the ability to make up their mind and this is a weakness to take advantage off. You should strive to play the role of bully or higher authority, someone who makes decisions for them. Provided you play up your best decisions while hiding your worst, you are bound to stay in their lives and stay in control.

- **Altruism:** This is one of those traits that are present in people who show a high level of honesty, fairness and empathy, emphasis on the empathy. This is the emotion to go after as it blinds the target to your true nature and makes him more likely to buy into your act. This makes he/ she susceptible to your talents but not foolish, so you'd still have to play your cards right to have the desired impact.

There are many other traits to look out for and with time and experience, you'd discover them. Looking closely, you would notice that at least one of these traits is present in everyone you know. This is the reason why everyone, even yourself can be manipulated and as such, while playing your game, never drop your guard and always be on the lookout in case your target is also playing a game on you. I should also add that while these traits make people more susceptible to manipulation, your abilities and skills are the factors that would truly determine if the manipulation would be successful or not.

Warning signs

Everybody can be manipulated but some people are less likely to fall than others. If you are a beginner and you are just learning the ropes, it is necessary for you to avoid individuals high up on the 'less likely' list. To achieve this, you need to know the particular traits or character types to look out for. Such people are:

- **The stubborn:** They are not impossible to break but are better avoided because they might cost too much effort. Stubborn people are usually hard to manipulate because they have self-created opinions, whose tenets they uphold strictly. Worse is the fact that they are prone to arguing a lot and seeing as this is rather inherent in them, it is a trait you would have to figure a way around if you plan on sticking around. Except you are very confident you can get the job done, steer clear.

- **Insensitive people:** This type lacks the ability to feel much in terms of empathy or sympathy and only care about their own interests. You might think that's a good thing but remember, their wellbeing is most likely top of their worries and any sign of manipulation is sure to set off alarm bells.

- **Immature people:** Immaturity is normally a trait that should set people out for manipulation because it is a close sibling of naivety. However, most immature people possess the ability to hold grudges for a tremendous period of time and you do not want them hunting you down for hurting their feelings or stealing their properties. They tend to make very determined enemies. The stubborn also possess this tendency.

- **People with close friends and relatives:** The best targets are usually those who reside far away from most family and friends because this reduces the chances of trusted outside forces trying to undo your work. Unless, you can think of a way to wean your target off such influence or at least factor them into your plans, the ploy is going to be extremely difficult to pull off. Even if you are ready to manipulate the entire group, ask yourself if it is worth the effort.

Chapter 5

Persuasion: the psychological theories (NEVER FAIL TO CONSIDER THE TARGET)

Persuasion is a deliberate effort to change or alter a person's opinions, beliefs or attitude toward a particular issue, situation, object or person. This is usually achieved by transmission of a message which could be verbal or symbolic.

While persuasion could be used in a manipulative sense, it is in actual sense different from manipulation. This is because, when persuading a person, he/she is usually aware of your efforts at changing their point of view and willingly or reluctantly allows you to try. In this instance, the person listens and concentrates on what you are saying and then tries to rationalize your ideas with reality before then putting whatever conclusions they come to comparison with what they previously believed.

Your role in the entire dynamic is to state your reasons for the change you are prescribing, give illustrations and evidence supporting your views and try to convince the target of your advances that your line of action or advice is their best bet. The main goal of this is getting them to switch to a state of reasoning or a product that you prefer. It is in this that persuasion resembles manipulation. Because your goal is still to push the target towards an outcome that they might ordinarily not have considered right.

The success attained in persuasion usually depends on the preconceptions held by the target and their strength, their perception of the person sharing the new message or idea, their perception of the message or idea and finally, their perception of the conclusion on offer. Upon outlining these reasons, it should be clear to you that the subject of your effort would probably possess ideas that are at least dissimilar, if not contradictory, to yours and as such the entire process would either hinge on your persuasion being very convincing or the ability of the target to meet a compromise between the conflicting ideas that would majorly mirror the changes you want.

Below are six major theories that strive to explain the way the human mind absorbs and reacts to information. Knowledge of these would greatly increase the odds of persuasion if you could pinpoint it in your target.

- **The attribution theory:** This concludes that people would either attribute actions and characters to people and object respectively either in relation to the context they are being considered in or according to their own emotional disposition.

  When they attribute using context as a guide, they are likely to come to decisions that take into consideration environment of origin and situational factors. Such is seen when a person refrains from calling a product inferior or calling a person insensitive, instead arguing that the product has been made from the best possible items available to the manufacturer and that the person is simply reacting as he has learnt to from his childhood environment.

However, when considering their own emotional disposition, they tend to believe that whatever is convenient for them is the only right decision or approach for every other person. Consider this situation:

You meet a person at an event or gathering and try starting a conversation with them but instead of giving you a polite audience, the person appears preoccupied with their own thoughts or acts aloof. Angered or annoyed, you walk away and when asked for an opinion on the person, you characterize them as proud, arrogant or self-important.

In this case, the characterization you have concluded on is based solely on your emotional disposition and does not take into consideration, the situation or possible problems the other person might have. The idea is not to determine whether or not you are wrong or right but rather to analyze how you are likely to process information about people and things. You actually might be right about the person.

Another situation is when you have been accused of doing something wrong and you claim that your accusers have failed to see things from your own perspective and are only interested in their own point of view.

This is a perfect example of considering things as regards context. In this case, probably because the things said are negative, you'd notice the emphasis placed on contextual understanding of actions. There is also a slight hint of the dispositional thinking occurring simultaneously.

- **The conditioning theory**: In this case, the person is likely to do things if they are tailored and conditioned to look like their own decisions instead of as a result of coercion. This is most utilized in the advertising industry where commercials, advertisements and billboards are used to convey information that would provoke positive feelings in the population of interest. They then connect such feelings to their products thus making you feel that the product would bring such a feeling into your life. Because of this, you are more likely to purchase their product, thinking all the while that your decision was an independent one.

  This is usually possible because we generally perceive things based on our emotions and are more likely to buy things because they make us feel good.

- **The cognitive dissonance theory**: Based on this theory, it is assumed that people tend to aim for consistency in their thoughts, attitudes and decisions. This is the reason why most people create principles which they strive to follow. Most people also seem intent on reconciling the contradictions as much as they can until they feel comfortable. I would give two examples on this.

Example 1

You have a very strong and deep-rooted need for canned food, either due to the laziness of having to cook meals or the frustrations at having to wait in queues for food. Then you are told that such canned meals could lead to cancer and you definitely don't want to have cancer. But you also don't want to stop eating canned food. So, instead of stopping with the habit, you comfort yourself that millions of people like you have the same habit and would never have cancer.

The cancer theory might be untrue but your eagerness to dispute the fact or at least to make the consequences seem less severe is your own way of changing your mind or at least making the facts you have just learned seem less important or true. This is one of the ways of dealing with cognitive dissonance theory.

Example 2

Imagine a criminal with a conscience. This is probably hard to imagine but they do exist. In such a situation, his or her criminal tendencies are clashing with their tender hearts and causing a bit of discomfort. Such a person is very likely dealing with his/ her problems by giving in to the rationale that a criminal and wealthy life far outweighs the benefits of having a clean conscience or good heart.

Again, I am refraining from judging whether such a rationale is sound but am more focused on the fact that the person seems to give in to a rationale that overlaps with the general aim of most people to deal with his discomfort. This is another way of dealing with the cognitive dissonance.

- **The judgement theory:** This one is very simple to grasp. It simply proposes that when faced with a new piece of information or idea a person's reaction is more or less dependent on the way he/she currently feels on the topic. What this means is that were likely to accept something that resonates with our current belief, reject something that doesn't fit in with our beliefs, or stay indifferent to something never previously considered.

Therefore, when attempting to persuade a person, it is better to first determine their views on the topic to gauge whether or not you'd be successful and if your effort would eventually be worth it.

- **Inoculation theory:** The inoculation theory supports the view that even if previously uninterested in two points of view, once argued for, you are likely to pick the dominant point of view and stick with it. Here is an example of what I mean.

You have never watched a game of soccer in your life but one day you are relaxing on the beach and happen to find yourself stuck between two diehard soccer fans, who support rival teams. An argument begins about whose team is better and more dominant and they both turn to you, presenting their points like you are s seasoned fan and after some time ask you to judge on who's better. You obviously would pick the person with the better argument so as not to betray your own lack of knowledge on the subject. If in future another individual was to pose a question to you, inquiring as to which of those two teams is better, you'd probably find yourself arguing in favor of the choice you made then, maybe even with some of the same points that were used then.

This is the power of inoculations, the most powerful initial idea always takes root first.

- **Narrative persuasion theory:** From experience, I think we would all accept that stories have a more enhanced effect on perception and opinions than abstract advice. The attitudes and opinions of people towards objects and others tend to change when they are told compelling stories of such subjects.

The theory simply attempts to explain the heightened effect can have on people if utilized properly. In this, the listener feels transported and this greatly affects their perception of events, making them more pronounced and vivid than they might have been if they had been expressed ordinarily and abstractly.

The psychological perspective

Ordinarily, persuading people would be difficult without the ability to properly organize and present an argument. But if inexperience in any or both of this is coupled with an inability to gauge and understand moods and stances, your task would be made many times more likely to fail.

The ability to instantly sense and recognize a person's stance on an issue is difficult, not to talk of performing the same trick on an audience. Because of this difficulty, most speakers who are attempting to introduce people to a new point of view always tend to ask questions that would enable them gauge the stance of the audience before moving on with their presentation.

Immediately after asking such questions, they usually watch out for visible reactions from members of the audience, maybe a smile to indicate a previous knowledge of the topic, sitting up to indicate interest, turning away or sighing to indicate disagreement or boredom or even a person willing to answer. These simple markers give you an idea as to how your message may be received and would help you map out a strategy of approach. It is also an effective tool as people tend to express themselves more sincerely when they do not feel particularly in the spotlight. So, if you are unsure, do not refrain from asking a few surface questions to test the waters or more aptly, to feel out the crowd.

It should also be noted that many people might give a negative reaction to one-on-one persuasion and would start arguments to further their points. The moment you realize that your attempt to persuade a particular person has deteriorated into an argument, it is advisable for you to walk away. Very few arguments occurring outside law courts ever get settled. Engaging in one would be fruitless and time consuming. That time is better spent elsewhere.

I stated earlier that manipulation is similar to persuasion in that both aim to change opinions, attitudes and actions from what they might have been to whatever you prefer and I had also stated that they differ from one another in that, persuasion is a more direct form of securing the change you desire, while manipulation requires you to operate in secret using emotional exploitation. Now, I would like to expatiate on the relationship between manipulation and persuasion or rather how persuasion can be adopted as a tool for manipulators.

This is not rocket science and needs only a simple alteration in approach to persuasion. It would require you to couple the ability to make compelling, irrefutable arguments with your ability to recognize emotional markers. Once both are in sync, you are ready to move. But why this two? The answer to that is rather simple. If you recognize an emotion to be dominant in the target and fell the need to convince, he or she to do something without outright manipulation, most likely due to the presence of friends and family, wouldn't it be better to play on such an emotion and use it as a leverage or platform with which you propel your point of view rather than just riding in without a strategy.

This is why persuasion makes manipulation look humane and might even reduce the noticeability of your ploy. It enables the manipulator, you, to touch on the emotions of a target for a reaction, but instead of making your telling moves under a shroud all the time, you adopt clever arguments and let them do the convincing for you. The trick however, is to always get the emotion right.

Chapter 6

Persuasion: The practical

In the previous chapter, I touched upon persuasion as a whole, focusing on the definition, its differences and similarities with manipulation as well as their relationship and how they could be adapted to work to your benefit as a manipulator. Other than that, the means by which the human mind absorbs and relates to new information and facts was also discussed. Now, I wish to approach how the theories of information absorption can be used to your advantage in real life situations. I want to give you practical tips on how to persuade people to do your bidding effectively.

Putting the theories into practice

The theories from the previous chapter were very explanatory regarding how people are most likely to relate with information but said very little about how to take advantage of their tendencies. This should give more detailed tips and tactics as to how the theories can be used maximally in real life situations as well as the groups of people most likely to possess each attribute.

- **Use of the attribution theory:** This theory manifests in all people but is more noticeable in pseudo manipulators or arrogant people. Such people are less likely to ever accept being wrong and are more likely to blame it on perspective instead. Here is an example on hoe to deal with such people.

Your target is a pseudo manipulator, one who likes to feel in control and powerful, and the roles in the relationship are already well defined. If on a given occasion such a person were to shut down your views in a bid to bully you into submission. You could use such an opportunity to play for something you need. Firstly, you have to avoid arguing your point for too long or too strongly. Always put up a little resistance to emphasize their power over you. Once he/she has lapsed into the role you want for them, ask them for tips on how to do what they want from you. Be sure to keep them talking, constantly asking questions and subtly driving the conversation towards your need. When they are at the their most vulnerable, they would be ready to do anything just to keep emphasizing their power.

The thing about such targets is that they are convinced of their powers over you and believe themselves to be infinitely smarter. People who think themselves smart love nothing more than giving lectures, in which your only role is to listen and ask more questions. Once you have got them talking for an extended period, proceed to move them in your direction of interest and when they appear to feel at their most powerful, they are likely to grant it without much consideration, much like the kings of old.

- **Use of the conditioning theory:** In a real-life situation, this theory involves using your wit and humor to flatter the target into believing whatever you want them to. It also makes them more likely to consider your suggestions. This follows the general principle that you would aim to acquire more of what pleases you and in this case who. A typical example is the confident guy who prides himself on being able to pick up a different girl every night. How does he do it? He simply wows and impresses them with a combination of humor, wit, an interesting conversation and a smoothness and style that is very difficult to recreate. He basically makes them feel good for five minutes at the bar and they believe he would make them feel equally as good for the entire night and therefore, happily follow him out. Though this works on almost everyone, naïve people are bound to be more success.

- **Use of the cognitive dissonance theory:** this is a generally difficult theory to use because, the onus is usually on the targets to make all the difference on their lives. But, if properly played, and you act as the adviser and close friend who gives the alternative idea or compromise that helps them deal with their dissonance, it makes you a sort of confidante. This gives you a choice position in their lives as from their point of view, you understand them more than any other person. This is, however, the sort of relationship that must be cultivated for a period of time before making your move.

- **Use of the judgement theory:** People rich in self-confidence, arrogant and who consider themselves smarter than most tend not to listen to or take into consideration arguments of other that are contradictory to their own views. If such people are to be persuaded, the new opinions they are to be inoculated with have to be similar to their previous ones or else all hopes would of persuading them would be impossible.

If you are to ever convince them that what they believe is wrong or inferior to yours, you need to make it feel that acceptance is their idea and not a necessity. The first step would be to pander to them, to defer slightly to their intelligence. Next, you draw similarities between your idea and theirs. When it comes to convincing, you are better served by an indirect approach where you ask questions and wait for them to answer, before gently expressing your objections, making sure to always be gentle and let their thought processes do the job of convincing them. It could be a change of opinion or a need to persuade them that a course of action better serves their interests, this method is sure to soften them up better than arguing with them.

Consider that friend who sees himself or herself as an authority on every subject regardless of how little knowledge they actually possess on the issue and remember how such people almost never back out of arguments but instead keep going at it till the environment of the discussion becomes toxic.

We have all had this kind of friend and the mistake of arguing with them even makes it harder for them to ever change their views. This is because, once they have taken a public stance an opinion, it is difficult for them to ever take another or even act against what they have supported, even if they later see more sense in your own view. This is because, going back on their belief is against their sense of pride and their ego. Thus, persuading such people is better done in private, if anything, because it gives you a chance to try again if you fail the first time. It also gives them a chance to adopt your idea in public without looking weak or stupid.

- **Use of the inoculation theory:** This is easy to utilize because almost everyone is susceptible to this. The key is making sure the person as no previous beliefs or opinions on the issue at hand. That is the only criterion. Once you are sure of this, you explain to them the advantages of your views. Never forget to also share the disadvantages but do this in a way that it doesn't affect the message you want them to have. The reason why the disadvantages must be made clear is that if they associate what you have explained to them with lies later along the line, they are very likely to change their views as a whole. So, if you need such people for the long term, make sure they have the full gist. Always emphasize the advantages and play down the disadvantages but never conceal them. This is as such, less a matter of persuading a person as it is initiating belief in them. For this reason, knowledge and utilization of this theory could be very powerful in the right situations. Such a situation is when you find yourself pitching a unique and previously utilized business idea in a meeting or when trying to preach a new doctrine, be it religious, academic or technological.

- **Use of the narrative persuasion theory:** The power of stories is well known. If you doubt it, all you have to do is think about how evangelists and religious clerics preach their messages. Are you getting the idea now? Though I should probably say that these clerics are probably among the most trained persons in the art of persuasion Because at one point they make use of so many theories of persuasion, constantly changing their tactics to better fit your fears and worries. But, enough with the clerics. The narrative persuasion theory is perhaps the most effective at persuading people because it involves giving them a story, a character that they could relate to and then relying on that story to do your convincing. Such a story might be true or if you are very talented, made up.

It really doesn't matter as long as you can get them to listen. It might not work every time when used alone but if you were to mix it up with other theories, just like the clerics, the chances of success are better.

Other techniques of persuasion

Persuasion, like manipulation, possesses guidelines on how best to achieve your aim. These guidelines could be treated as strategies or tactics and would increase your chances of success the more you get used to them. The faster, the better.

- **Use of force:** The use of force or aggression could be effective or not and more often than not, it is a win or nothing tactic. It involves not a lot of coaxing but a lot of demanding and as such, if the person or audience don't dig the vibe, there is no other means of retreating. It usually involves use of statements that sound threatening and would most likely be a good fit for dealing with people with low self confidence and sense of self-worth. Also note that if the idea is to impress friends and family of your target, it would be better if this tactic were used in private beyond the hearing or view of other parties as it could easily be perceived as bullying.

- **Commitment and consistency:** These are highly respected values in the minds of most people in all walks of life. When coupled with a little bit of success, it could be very effective if not the most effective means of persuasion. If you want someone to believe your way is gold and your opinions are equally as rich, there is no better way than providing an example of their successes. In most cases, the best example is usually yourself. Showing commitment to your ideals and consistently applying them successfully tends to convince people of their truthfulness. It eliminates the need for you to continue arguing your points regularly, instead let them persuade themselves that following your example is the right thing. It would be like seeing a successful person and emulating them in the hopes that you'd achieve their level of success the same way. We all do it, so why not use it to our advantage when dealing with others.

Another angle to this, could be to get the target to commit themselves to promises or writing. This would be useful because most people care about reputations and rarely want to be seeing going back on their words. While this second angle would be an effective tool on arrogant people and pseudo manipulator, the first method is more likely to work for people lacking in confidence and self-esteem.

- **Social influence:** Social influence could manifest in one of two ways. It could be positive or negative. Positive influence would point to the need for one to follow the convention or approach that is the most common around him/her or among friends. The negative influence, on the other hand deals with the tendency of people to act against the norm. The influence that is expressed is usually deep rooted and expresses itself in more than one fact of the target's life. Once the targets tendency has been established, you could move to surround the person only with people who possess the approach that would produce the result you desire. This method is also applicable to people with a low sense of self-esteem and confidence.

- **Action by reciprocity:** reciprocity generally means the need or tendency to give back when you are given something. You are probably wondering how this affects persuasion, right? This is straightforward. Giving something creates the need in the target to give back. This in turn is a weakness that makes the target more susceptible to catering to a need that they otherwise could have overlooked. This is also applicable to arrogant people as well as those who possess altruistic dispositions. An empathetic person is also likely to fall for such a ruse. This could also be used or claimed to be used subliminally, as most times you need not even state the need verbally or outrightly but instead subtly imply to its absence.

- **Use of authority or sternness:** If the target is a naïve person or one who is lacking in decisiveness or assertiveness, this is the ideal method of approach. This is for people who are prone to listening to other people's opinions and taking it for the truth, especially when they consider the person to be more of an authority on the subject than they are. It would also help if they consider your views trustworthy and knowledgeable. This is the method of choice when dealing with a new or junior colleague or at least someone who is new to an environment and is not yet well versed in how things operate. However, treating such people could also be counterproductive, causing them to view you in a negative light.

- **Taking advantage of love:** It might be a simple crush or a big attraction, but people almost always say yes to people they like and feel something positive for. So, if you have a target that you feel is attracted to you, play their feelings to your advantage and ask for whatever you want, just be careful to give a little back and do not overdo it. If the person is emotionally dependent on you, your luck is strong because they are even less likely to utter a word for fear of losing you to another. The best part is that they never realize that such is happening, as it is a very natural reaction.

- **Leveraging your trust and integrity:** if you are generally acknowledged to be trustworthy, you are more likely to be believed. This could be done by smartly showing off your impeccable reputation, if you have one, while avoiding the line of arrogance. That could spoil the effect. Another way to use this tactic is to put your character in the spotlight, if you have a good one, and making sure to back up your every point with a vow of assurance in its trustworthiness.
  The last is to give a sense of expertise. Show that you possess more knowledge than they do and when added to your reputation and character, you have a cocktail of persuasion that even the most steadfast of non-believers would reconsider. It is also likely to work on naïve people and people who consider themselves intellectual.

- **Making use of sympathy and empathy:** These two emotions can easily be manipulated because they usually convey on their owners, a sense of innocence and docility that can be used against them. With the right words and gestures, you should be able to convince such people of anything. For a more advanced effect, make use of stories as such people are also prone to following the narrative transportation theory and the combination of these two factors make them better candidates to believe than most.

Reverse psychology

Reverse psychology is a technique of persuasion where a speaker or person utilizes a behavior or idea that is contradictory to that which he wants to occur. The user of this technique does or asks for the opposite of what they actually require of the target, encouraging the target to do as they wish.

This works on people who make a habit of resisting authority. If tried on people who are more agreeable, they might and would probably do as you have asked. For this reason, they do not make good candidates or targets for reverse psychology to be used upon.

However, even when used with resistant people, reverse psychology should be used as subtly as possible because no one enjoys or likes being manipulated and as such, if they recognize what you are doing, it is likely you would not achieve much with them. An example of the use of reverse psychology is advising someone to do something when you know that the very idea of the advice infuriates him/her and would probably push them towards doing the opposite. The idea is usually to establish the idea you actually want them to absorb then play it up subtly to become tempting, before changing tack and arguing against it. Immediately after this, you push them to make a decision and that's all. It is likely that they would go with it because other than the fact that they would want to resist the advice, it is also the idea that they were exposed to first. It is not necessary to take such steps if you know the person well enough to understand what they like, dislike and how they would react in given situations.

Remember to always analyze before making your move

The reason why most people fail in persuading people into a line of action is that they fail to grasp what is necessary for their success and if they do, they fail to take it all into consideration. It is for this same reason that persuading strangers is more difficult than persuading people you are closer to. Because if you were to ignore a person's emotional disposition and shelf their possible reactions, it would be the same as approaching a stranger. To really succeed at persuasion, most times you might need to adopt maybe a dominant, authoritative attitude or a more reserved one.

When being authoritative, you have to give off a vibe of knowledgeability and confidence. You must convince the person that you know what you are speaking about, while emphasizing their own knowledge. There is a loophole here. If this is tried on a resistant person, he or she is likely to do the opposite of what you advise and thus fall a victim of reverse psychology. You see that knowledge of the person is important in determining the best technique for persuasion for without it, you would be charging blindly.

You should also avoid using reverse psychology very often as such misuse could expose your tricks and make the target more immune to your ministrations. It could be particularly damaging to relationships and you do not want this, unless that in itself is your goal. If you are to use reverse psychology, always remember to stay smart and stay calm. Do not let your emotions control you but, just like in manipulation, control your emotions.

Persuasion is an art that all socially influential people crave possession of. This is because the ability to make people do as you wish and while you can directly manipulate individuals, it becomes trickier when dealing with groups of people. But if you were to master this art, your power and influence would benefit greatly.

Chapter 7
Common manipulation techniques

At a point in our life, and at least once daily for most, we resort to manipulation to get what we want. It could be a little lie to get out of a tight spot or harmless flattery to get yourself a choice seat but it is manipulation. So, stop believing that manipulation is an art reserved for only the evilest of people, everyone does it so it's simply better to get very good at it. Though it is better to look out for some traits that predispose some to manipulation more than others, it doesn't mean that people without such traits can't be played.

I have previously elaborated on such traits as well as other means of gaining control over people but it's time to approach the real topic of discussion, how to manipulate people.

Lying

This is the most popular of all manipulation techniques. On its own, lying is simply misinforming the target or at the most, concealing information from the target but when done with a view to controlling people, it becomes a pretty powerful weapon. Consider lying as a tool to soften up a target that has until that moment proven too strong. Lying in this way would require one to betray the very intent of conventional lying because in this case, you are not trying to misinform or conceal but rather to confuse.

If you are to succeed at this, your lies need to be believable and contradictory at first. At the beginning of such a ploy, it is necessary for your lies to constantly bounce of each other, creating a means through which you could sow seeds of confusion in someone who is usually sure of themselves.

Consider lying to a partner about a past relationship. Then in a later discussion on a similar topic, drop a previously thought of slip-up that contradicts the first experiences you shared with them. The target might not notice this at first and may require a few more similar lies before the inconsistencies start to call their attention but when it does, instead of defending yourself, clam up and play the victim. Tell a sob story about emotional pain and all of that; share with them the reason for your lies. The stories and reasons might be fictitious, but the more realistic the better. So, be sure to think everything through first.

In this sort of scenario, the initial contradicting lies are needed to throw a seemingly strong person off balance. There is nothing like a perfect person or a truly balanced person and, as such, regardless of how strong we might seem on the outside, we all have weaknesses and there is no better way to start the process of exposing someone's emotional vulnerabilities than forcing them to instigate a heart to heart moment or discussion. If you were to try creating such a moment on your own, the target would still be likely to stay closed. However, if such a discussion is their idea, whatever barriers they possessed, they would have brought down by themselves. That is the goal with this lie.

It puts you in a position to change the narrative. In a situation in which the power was previously balanced in most of your relations, making yourself seem weak or vulnerable could put the target in an uncomfortable position and force them into opening up to adapt to their new role. Just be sure to keep any contradictory lies out of your final story. While this might not bring you much in terms of favors, having them belief you opened up on some deep secret to them strengthens their attachment. they feel a stronger bond has been formed. This trick is likely to work on people who are emotionally secure and need to believe you are really open with them before they can open up.

Punishment

When I say punishment, I do not mean physical abuse or violence. No, I mean resorting to tactics like the silent treatment, nagging, shouting or mood swings. I know you are probably thinking how any of these behaviors could get you any control but if you learn to selectively release such emotions and actions at the right time, they could exert just the right effect on the target.

The silent treatment for example could be used to put the right person in a state of wanting to please you. This treatment is a popular one for manipulators when dealing with assertive people as well as people with low self-confidence. In such case, you create a fictional quarrel in your head that need not have happened in reality. All it needs to be is believable and offensive from your perspective. Then follow through with the silent treatment. When the target gets desperate to get you back to your former self, drop the act and ask for whatever you wish for. This is a direct technique that might not always work but for a beginner, it is worth a try and for an expert, if partnered with the right set of skills and ploys, its chances of success become better.

Remember when you were little and your parents tried keeping you away from the candy or cookie jar and instead of throwing a tantrum and crying, you just stalked back to your room, threw the sheets over your head and refused to talk to anybody. You wait for hours determined not to make the first move and, later at night your parents come into the room, bearing gifts and treats and maybe even the promise of a trip you want.

Not all children did this but most did and yes, children manipulate too. They might not recognize it for what it is but they actually do it and since it works, they keep resorting to it again and again. The best thing about such a ploy is at the exact instance during which it occurs, the target believes that they are doing the right thing to keep you happy and keep the relationship from dying.

If nagging were to be the strategy of choice for you. Be sure the target is either one who lacks assertiveness or one who is eager to please because such people are likely to react favorably to nagging. Let's say you want something badly, all you have to do is keep asking and asking until they give in. Due to their lack of assertiveness, through all the asking, they would probably never give you an outright no for an answer and if it is a target who is always eager to please, he or she would have begun considering the pros and cons from the second time you ask and with just a little extra push, they would cave.

Mood swings are another very effective strategy in unbalancing a target. They are just more negative than lying and if utilized, care has to be taken to avoid dwelling too much or for too long on negative emotions such as anger. rather, it would be better to spend more time in a neutral state of boredom or indifference. The trick behind utilizing mood swings is to make your target associate some actions of theirs with particular moods of yours. This would give them an idea about what you like and dislike without you uttering a word. It is thus, advised to use this tactic alongside a more reserved attitude.

Imagine your roommate tends to leave their dishes undone after a meal, you do something drastic like throwing such plates in the trash and then refrain from talking much about it for that night but when you wake the next morning, you adopt a lighthearted demeanor and refuse to lower the smile regardless of what he or she does.

The next time, your roommate invites someone over without informing you and you act in a similar way. You never let your reactions slip over into the next day and other than when the target does something you find offensive, never react in such a way. Also, make sure that you do this only rarely.

Depending on the type of person your roommates is he or she would react differently. If the person is naive or is lacking in self-esteem, they would pander to you and fail to repeat whatever it is you reacted to but if the person is insensitive, your reactions would probably not do the trick and you would have to resort to another tactic.

Sarcasm and flattery

While other techniques mentioned earlier have dealt with manipulation using actions and acting, if you are good with words, this is a more likely weapon for you. The power of words is often underexaggerated in favor of actions. However, if mastered, they could be just as useful if not more.

Sarcasm and flattery are two slightly contrasting techniques that could be used to control the actions and opinions of people. They are usually most effective on someone who lacks self-esteem. Such a person is likely to believe most negative and positive things you say about them and start working to please you. Because of this, you could use sarcasm to deliver well planned putdowns whenever such a person offends you, only to resort to flattery to increase their confidence. Such polarity on such a week mind means they would cling to you for the compliments and flattery and would start doing things only to please you even if it goes against their own needs.

The applications of sarcasm and flattery lose all or at least most of their effectiveness if they are blatantly employed. To avoid these you must understand the need for subtlety. In the case of sarcasm, the very idea is for you to be blatant in your execution while subtly hiding your goal. You must make whatever comment you deem fit without making the target feel as if you are directing them towards a particular line of action. Failing at this could have the alternate effect of making them immune to you.

When you were young, you probably associated bullies with violence, shoving people into lockers and all but you should be able to point out that person who always alternated in behavior, showing you his or her good parts on one day, only to switch it up the next. The person would have been so polarizing that people were often confused about whether they loathed or loved him or her and with time would start to find that they hovered around such people, trying to cater to their every need. Do you recognize them now? You probably had a few in your high school and most times they were really popular.

Two of the most effective tactics employed by those people were sarcasm and flattery. With subtle swipes of their tongues they could play down your happiest moment or your biggest achievement to be something worthless and in the next, they could make one of your more ordinary actions seem spectacular. As much as they hurt your feelings, you'd still find yourself doing things they would find pleasing whenever they were around.

This might have happened to you and it might not have but the very fact that it happened to some speaks volumes of the effectiveness of such tactics. So, never forget to destabilize a mark using sarcasm and flattery. Another advantage of these two techniques is that they keep you from having to resort to trickier aggressive or abusive techniques when slight words and gestures would do the trick perfectly.

Isolation

This is mostly a secondary tactic used to make sure no external forces mess with your manipulation. The presence of family and friends around the target provide an extra level of insulation or protection around the target as such people tend to call the target back on some of their actions when they get suspicious. Their presence there, whispering into the ear of the mark thus creates another source of influence, besides yours, whose sole purpose is to thwart your influence.

Whenever you get the target to fulfil a need for you such people would call he/she back and try to expose how you are manipulating them and that puts the ploy you have implemented in jeopardy.

On its own, isolation is not that effective but it is worth noting that in the absence of friends and family alike, the target starts to look onto you as their only source of advice, comfort, love, help etc. In other words, they become completely dependent on you emotionally and this heightens the level of control you possess over them. This in turn makes them easier to influence.

Guilt tripping and love bombing

These two are a very common duo used by manipulators but that doesn't in any way affect their effectiveness. Guilt tripping is when you manipulate your targets reactions making them feel guilty about doing particular things simply by playing on their emotional vulnerabilities. Naturally, guilt is a very uncomfortable feeling which most people strive to eliminate. This need to eliminate their guilt after an incident is what you should aim to take advantage of. Since such chances might be few and far between, the initiative to create situations that give you a platform on which you could leverage a person's guilt against them is on you. In such a case, the understanding of your targets emotions and what makes them tick comes into play. You need to know how you can make them feel guilty so as to take advantage of them and their guilt.

Consider a situation in which a partner or girlfriend refuses to accompany you to a company gathering. If the gathering is not important to you, you could clam up and use a mood swing to leverage them for something that is. But if you consider the gathering too important to miss or you need a plus one to impress a particular attendee and your partner is refusing. You could play the guilt card, making them feel selfish and unkind for not considering your needs. You would make yourself the victim, putting your partner in an awkward position where they feel like they are depriving you of something you need for their own selfish reason. When this is used on less assertive people or people lacking in self-confidence, the result is usually stunning as more often than not they end up doing exactly what you want. They might even outperform your expectations simply because of their need to eliminate the feelings of guilt you have created in them.

Using such a tactic, you rile up someone that loves or is attached to you by telling them and claiming that they do not care or are too selfish in the way they treat you. This would keep an emotionally vulnerable person in check, making them see you as the victim of their actions a rather than the other way around. They would then be eager to prove your claims wrong, thus, increasing in them the need to please.

Love bombing, on the other hand, is a technique in which you continuously and over an extended period of time shower a person with love, impressing them with charm while getting whatever you want from them. This is usually much difficult to tell apart from real love and that's what makes the mark even more vulnerable. Love bombing is effective on almost everyone because as humans we all love to feel good and this need drives our selection of the people we hang out with. If someone makes us feel loved and cared for, we impulsively strive to spend more time with them. This would also mean that the target would feel more inclined to satisfy your need in order to maintain his or her happiness. However, like most tactics, the effect of love bombing is more pronounced in some character types. What this means is that, depending on the level of love bombing you expose a target to, some would see it is as a result of you trying to be nice and would consider you a good friend while other would see your actions as more and would consider you as more than a friend.

Individually, love bombing and guilt tripping are effective but when combined they are devastating. I am yet to explain reinforcement but the effect they produce is quite similar. To achieve such an effect, you should probably expose the target to your loving and charming side. Make the effect of your love felt then when the moment is right, you withdraw it and leave the target craving for it. The next step is to up the ante by making them feel guilty about your withdrawal. You make them feel like your current mood and state is their fault and when you feel that they are ripe and ready to accommodate your whims and needs, you slowly slip back into the role of loving and caring for them.

Most of the time, this works and its success is because every time you put both ploys in play, you create a sort of hypersensitivity to your needs and wants in the target. You get them into a state a where all they want to do is return to the period of time when all you did was love them and charm them.

You might also resort to completely playing the victim just to make the target more uncomfortable and guiltier, softening them up for whatever it is that you actually want of them.

This is the technique used by con men and women who want to take advantage of vulnerable people and make some wealth for themselves in the process. They inveigle their way into the lives of such people and then love-bomb them to the point where, the target cannot imagine an extended period of time without them and would, for that reason alone, do anything to keep them happy. Whenever they fail to get their way, they would then resort to guilt tripping in order to bring the target back into a state of mind in which their major thought would be on pleasing them. It might seem odd and unbelievable but if you think about it long enough, you'd realize that these two are the most used techniques by gold diggers and emotional swindlers.

Reinforcement

This technique is easy to understand but hard to actually apply and as such is better learnt by trial and error. In this ploy, you provide the target with whatever he or she wants, be it money, gifts, sex or companionship, provided it is within your capability. And after the person grows accustomed to having what you give them, you begin the process of constantly withdrawing and providing them with these, constantly keeping them on their toes and making them vulnerable with you.

The major trick here is figuring out what the target wants, what makes them tick or what most tickles their ego. You have to identify that weakness that everyone has and reinforce it. It might be praise and recognition the person desires, give it to them. It might be money and gifts, give it to them. It might be sex or prestige, give it to them. But whenever you feel they are not conforming to your whims or are not taking care of your needs or are even daring to take you for granted, withdraw all that you have given to them and in a bid to get it all back, they would come groveling and begging. After the first time, they would probably learn to satisfy your every want if they don't want you withdrawing your reinforcement.

For example, there is at least a smidgen of materialism in all of us and this can be taken advantage of. If you meet a lady whose weakness lies in her love of material possessions and you have the money to spend, you are in luck. All you have to do is charm her, take her on a few shopping trips, spend your money on her and basically reinforce her love of material things. Upon every reinforcement, try upping the ante on the things you ask of her. You could start with insisting she spend more time with you, insisting she accompany you to any event you wish and with time you could try asking her or commanding her to stay over whenever you like. To keep up the supply of riches, love for which you have reinforced in her, she would most likely conform to your needs or at least beg for a reprieve rather than reject you. But if she seems to take your kindness for granted, kick her to the curb and withdraw your reinforcement. She is likely to come back hat in hand, apologizing for her behavior and eager to please.

Not to restrict this to only your love life, this technique could also be applied to almost any setting, including business, family relationships and any case in general provided there exist a means by which you reinforce the individual or group involved. If you think about it, you would notice that there really is little difference between this and parents who threaten to ground you and take away your freedom unless you behave as they wish or business men who pull out of deals with established customers in the hope of pushing them into making desperate, unfavorable deals that would benefit them.

In the case of the parents, they have reinforced your love of freedom by allowing you do the things you like most of the time. This, when coupled with our inherent need to be free, makes us eager to please them anytime they threaten to take that freedom away. Couple the love for freedom with the fact that they are your providers of everything you need and you would see that they have quite the hold on you.

As I implied earlier, manipulation is rife in the world and silently hoping for an ideal world in which it doesn't exist would make no difference. It is better you wizen up and get better at it than other before you are taken on a ride.

I left this as the last technique on my list because there is a possibility or rather, an inevitable reaction that you always have to take into consideration when dealing with people. This is ingratitude or sometimes boredom. People tend to take for granted things they can have all the time and over a long period of time, they are bound to get bored. To avoid this, you would need to be very good at utilizing multiple techniques at various times on the same target.

This ingratitude or boredom is most likely to occur when reinforcement is used and to counter this reaction you must understand that whatever you are reinforcing in the target could make them take you for granted. Because of this, you must always be ready to withdraw your reinforcement not only when they misbehave but also when you like to. This sounds mean and selfish and it actually is, but you need to know that for reinforcement to work, you need to be selfish. You have to make the target see your needs as being more important than theirs and to successfully do this, selfishness is necessary. The target needs to know that your efforts at making them feel good come at a price and the price is anything you want in return. Thus, being nice doesn't cut it here; you need to be mean sometimes to truly make it work for you.

Manipulation is not always for the faint hearted

Manipulation is not always wrong, nor is it always right but one thing that can be agreed upon is that it leaves an effect on both the user and the target. Depending on how manipulation was used, the effect might be positive or negative. Manipulation is usually used as a means of harming, subduing or using a person usually in a way that benefits the manipulator mostly at the expense of the target. The negative effects of manipulation are not experienced by the victim alone and in most cases, the users are not aware of the negative effects their behavior is having on their lives and, thus, become victims of their own manipulation. One of the problems of manipulation is the transfer or possession of power.

Power is naturally very addictive and very corrupting and so when faced with the question of what to use the power you have over people for, people tend to think about their selfish needs and how to make them happen. The idea of having power over a group of people or person is tempting and when such power is gotten it can lead to complete subordination and even abuse. While that is an effect on the victim, the user of such power might also become dependent on it thus making it difficult for them to have any sort of relationship with anybody unless they have power to exert. This can be damaging, both psychologically and emotionally, in the long run.

Chapter 8
Mastering the art of subtlety-DO NOT BE BLATANT

If manipulation isn't subtle, it probably wouldn't be effective. The very idea of manipulation thrives on the ability to subtly plant ideas, thoughts and opinions in the mind of the target and frame it in such a way that they believe that such ideas are the best they could come up with or the right thing to do.

Subtlety is necessary because the target has to feel that your every action is natural and actually not intended to influence them. This would mean that you first have to reduce the frequency with which you manipulate them. Manipulating them would mean reacting regularly in a negative way to what they do. This might seem unnatural to the target and could even lead them into believing that you are always trying to push on their buttons which, by the way, you are. The ability to be subtle is as important as the ability to read emotions because subtlety makes your knowledge of their emotions and reactions remain unknown to them.

Being blatant in the way you manipulate a person would also draw the attention of other people such as friends and family and, in all honesty, there is hardly a better way to put your manipulation of a target in jeopardy than exposing them to the influence of their family and friends. The simple secret to being subtle is to keep your judgements to yourself and keep your actions and reactions as cool and as undetectable as possible.

The cautious approach is always best

Regardless of how vulnerable a target might seem or how susceptible to manipulation they might look from a distance, it is necessary for you to approach the idea of manipulating a person cautiously. It isn't ever something to jump into just because of the possibility that the manipulation could be successful.

Cautiousness has to extend to all areas of the manipulation, from the planning to the approach and everything in between. This is especially important when dealing with strangers or people with whom you haven't spent that much time with. The emotions of such people are usually difficult to follow, even for the experts, and as such it is better to proceed with utmost caution at first and consolidate on the little progress you make.

The same thing applies when dealing with people you know because even though the chances of you getting it wrong is very slim, it still exists and for this reason you have to consider your actions before going on with them otherwise you risk destroying your relationships.

Another problem with throwing caution to the wind is that it exposes your tactics and your goal to the target. While some people might just cut you loose and move on with their lives, others might feel the need to expose you to a dose of your own medicine. Such people would probably try to manipulate you in return with a view at causing you pain. So, if the need to succeed does not make you cautious, maybe thinking about your own well-being does the trick.

A flimsy ploy is ineffective

Other than the ability to actually go through with the manipulation, another thing to pay attention to is the solidity of the ploy. This consists of details such as the rightness of the strategy to be utilized as regards the emotional and psychological disposition of the target as well as the situation in which you find yourself in.

The technique applied always has to seem like a natural reaction to whatever situation you find yourself in. If the reaction is unnatural, the ploy might still work out but if looked at closely, what you are doing would become more visible to the target and more so to outsiders who lack the emotional dependence the target has for you.

For this reason, no matter who the target is or how long the relationship has been going on for, you always need to make sure that the manipulation is foolproof and that no one is the wiser to your plans.

Scouting out the right target and putting the right approach into play would be useless if the general ploy is easily seen through. The ploy has to consist of you yourself, the image you are portraying to the target, how the role you are playing interacts with your actions and most importantly, the fluidity of the entire ploy. If any of this is found lacking or for some reason, the various elements are found to be out of sync with one another, the chances of success reduce considerably.

Never get ahead of yourself

The ability to keep yourself on track and put your mind to the task even when things are going well for you is an important attribute in every facet of life. Regardless of how well the relationship might be for you at a particular time or how much the manipulation is serving your interests, never ever lose track of yourself.

A loss of concentration could manifest in many ways. It could be a tendency for you to lose hold of your target, a need to avoid subtlety or the urge to fast-track a ploy. Any of these is risky as it exposes you to a better chance of failure, which in turn could lead to a complete breakdown of your plan. You must always stay alert to your surroundings and the reactions of your target to them. You must never fail to recognize how a situation affects a target or else you risk losing them prematurely.

Never go all out unless...

Subtlety is a rule most manipulators always conform to. The ones who choose to not obey this are often less successful and when they succeed, their success is usually short-lived. We have established the need for secrecy and subtlety but there are times when being subtle is disadvantageous or not as effective as being blatant. In these cases, you are advised to apply the needed pressure where necessary.

The ability to recognize when a situation requires more pressure than finesse as well as the best way to deliver such pressure is one garnered through experience and failure.

Situations that could call for the application of pressure are numerous but you must be able to determine if the pressure is actually necessary and how to apply it. One such situation is the need to keep a target when you feel they are slipping away.

For example, you have been working a target for a while. You have done everything by the book, maintaining isolation, staying on guard and generally looking out for any potential spoilers while getting what you want from the target. Then, in comes an old friend who is not so charmed by you. This friend goes on the attack, trying to pull the target from your clutches and you have really worked out to get to this point. You don't want to stop now. Then to bring your target back, you do something drastic like proposing marriage. This is the sort of pressure I am talking about.

In such a situation, you would agree that all other more subtle methods might and probably had already failed under such a spirited assault from the friend but instead of pulling out and walking away, you do the one thing that would express your desperation to keep the target close to you. Saying this here makes it look like showing desperation is a bad thing but from the point of view of the target, it convinces them of the truthfulness of your affection. If such a friend truly suspected of manipulation, she would have most likely used your avoidance of true commitment to prove her point and such an act would completely vilify their views and opinions in the eye of the target.

Chapter 9
Practical uses of manipulation

Manipulation as a tool is quite versatile as it does not particularly have any situations that it is restricted to. What this means is that, as long as people are involved in whatever you are involved in, be it a business setting, a relationship or whatever, manipulation can be used to further your agenda

Manipulation in business

the knowledge of manipulation and persuasion is critical if you plan to avoid being drawn into office politics not of your making or if you are out to avoid being cheated or railroaded by superiors and colleagues alike. Also, in business settings, there is a need for members of the same organization or group to confirm their views with one another and influence each other to cater to the group's interests. The ability to persuade people that your point of view is best would be quite handy in such a scenario.

Sales people also need to be well versed in the arts because most times they deal with people who believe them to be swindlers and for that reason they need to manipulate the persons perception of them, creating a positive one, before they could then begin the process of persuading such a customer to try out their products. there are some informal rules to follow when practicing manipulation in such business setting.

1. Don't push the limits: when I say limits, I do not mean yours, I mean that of the people you are manipulating. One of the ways that people punish the limit is by trying to manipulate everyone very time. While this might work effectively in a relationship, in an organization, everyone watches everyone closely and being associate with a tendency to manipulate people does not do your credibility much good. You have to be smart enough and disciplined enough to refrain from doing anything unless it is important. You have to always pick your battles well. If you overdo it and people start to view you as manipulator, they start to monitor your every move and even the most mundane of your actions become an object of intense scrutiny. Such scrutiny would make it a whole lot more difficult for you to achieve anything when it truly matters.

2. Sharpen your senses: Senses in this sense mean the ability to listen to and watch others. In a business setting, the ability to listen and perceive the disposition of others and so, when possible, say nothing, take a backseat and let others have the floor. Due to the fact that everybody in such a setting is always trying to get ahead of the next, it would be better if you could discern their strategies and goals, and there is no better way to achieve that by putting yourself in a position to hear and see everything.

3. Create a connection: Be it a customer or a colleague, you have to build a connection with them. Most people make the mistake of believing that they only need to build connections with their bosses but this line of action would only serve to paint you as your boss' stooge and alienate you from your fellow workers. on the contrary, forging a bond with both your colleagues and your bosses would make them see you as more of a bridge and less of a stooge. Another need for such a connection is the fact that you are more likely to be in the position to influence the thoughts and opinions of people when they feel they have a connection with you than if they consider you a complete stranger. This is particularly important when you are pitching an idea to others and its absence is the major reason why cold pitching is a very difficult trick to pull off.

4. Always stay neutral, when you can. in a business setting, neutrality should be your best strategy. Never take sides unless you have utmost confidence as to which side possesses more power. Taking sides early on would strip you of your flexibility and limit you to working only one angle. You must eb adept at playing both sides until you recognize which side would come out on top. The right way to maintain neutrality is to acknowledge the talents of everyone equally while also expressing real views regarding their failures. Other than strengthening your position of neutrality, such a tactic would also earn you the respect of everyone. However, like every other tactic you have to know when to apply this and this knowledge would be the difference between you successfully holding you position or even advancing in the ranks and you ailing spectacularly.

Manipulation in relationships

Manipulation ion relationships is the one society is most sensitive about. If you manipulate in the office, most people, outsiders, would view it a s a general tactic used by many in the same situation, but manipulating in a relationship is in the eye of most, a negative marker on the character of the manipulator. Regardless of whether your intentions are pure or selfish, this opinion does not change and it is for this reason that whatever plan you have for a spouse or close friend must be done in utmost secrecy. This brings us to a previously stated point, isolation.

Isolation is one of the most important factors to be considered if you want your manipulation of a person to be successful. You must wean the target off their family and friends, establishing yourself as their confidante and emotional companion. This is because the external influence exercised by such people is capable of rivalling that which you have created and rendering your plans a waste of time.

Another thing to pay attention to is your intention. You must be disciplined, check yourself and make sure that your needs from the target do not morph into complete selfishness. You must learn to control and wield the power you possess over them with caution and with sense to avoid causing them harm. This is only possible if you think beyond your own needs and ask yourself if your need might lead to any negative consequences for the target and if so, how serious such consequences would be. Manipulation is a very powerful tool and should be treated as such.

Manipulating a friend

Of all settings for manipulation, this is the most popular and the least suspicious or revolting. Manipulating a friend is so common, we barely pay attention to it. It usually manifests when we want to get information or something out of one another.

The best and easiest method of manipulating friends is through the use of reciprocity and compliments. Sometimes we do favors for friends because we want to but we also grant difficult favors not because we want to but because we recognize that we might need something equally as difficult to grant in the future. You do not always have to do big things, it might be a couple of smaller favors, but having them in the bag means you could leverage on reciprocity later in the future. Beware of insensitive or particularly selfish people, because they tend to not conform to reciprocity except it favors them in the moment.

The use of compliments is another way by which we unknowingly and harmlessly manipulate ourselves. The compliment might be sincere or insincere but when we give them, we recognize that they make our friends feel better about whatever it is they might have done, making them more likely to make us feel better too, whether by returning such compliments or by other means.

Offering support sort of falls under reciprocity but it is still valid as a standalone point. We might argue that offering our support to our friends in arguments and in their time of need is the right thing to do but even when we think they are wrong, we rarely ever withdraw our support. why? This is because, when we have arguments or times when we need support, we recognize the need to have someone in our corner and who better than someone who we offer unconditional support to when they need it. You can see that the manipulation is usually unintentional and harmless, but it is still a manipulation because if faced with the same choice when another person is involved, such a friend would probably do what they feel is right and not what you need. In this way, you can see that the need to reciprocate the support you showed has altered their behavior and reactions.

Seductive manipulation

Like cleopatras manipulation of both Julius Caesar and Mark Anthony, this involves using your sexuality and possible sexual prowess as a tool in getting whatever it is you need from a target. While this is an effective method, it also doesn't last that long if you can't get the target to develop more tangible feelings for you.

The truth is that there is a limit to how long sex can hold a person down and because of this, it is better to initially play hard to get. This has the double effect of making them mistake their lust for a more potent feeling while also pushing them to impress you just to get closer to achieving their target, which is having you. The key is in the timing. You have to be able to realize when the target might be losing interest and also recognize the steps you have to take to reignite their interest. Finally, you have to know when to give in. It would be better for your ploy if you have the sexual prowess to match your games as this would make you less of a pretender and more of the real deal.

If properly played, a game of seductive manipulation could lead to real feelings and would thus make the target even more dependent on you. Everyone is susceptible to this sort of manipulation because we all crave emotional and physical relationships with others regardless of how small the urge is.

How to properly manipulate strangers

Strangers are the hardest to manipulate or persuade because you usually have no idea how they think, how they process information or what makes them tick. In fact, most of the time, when you approach a stranger you find yourself following your instincts and searching for a foothold in their minds that you can leverage into a real connection. This is the smart way to go when dealing with individuals you barely know but such a method is slow and could end up being frustrating.

The alternative is quicker, riskier and used mostly by pick up artists. It is one in which you walk up to the target and impress he or she with an intoxicating mix of charm, wit and the promise of a very interesting future. This plan could fall by the wayside if your version of humor doesn't click with theirs or if your target is in the wrong state of mind for your ploy to have an effect.

Another way is to go all out and state what you want. This is rarely utilized, mostly because it betrays the very essence of manipulation; secrecy and emotional control. It is also rarely successful, so unless you are feeling lucky or the universe seems to be in your corner, don't try it.

Chapter 10
Manipulating and Scouting: The Forgotten Connection

I like to compare the game of manipulation to the hunting rituals of a predator while hunting a prey. When hunting prey, the lions of the African savannah watch their unfortunate prey - say a herd of wildebeests grazing in the distance. The lions (usually a pride) lie in wait, studying the unsuspecting prey, analyzing the herd and seeking out the weak and the vulnerable of the herd, pretty much scouting the herd. After successfully picking a target, the lions then plan a mode of attack, assigning the roles of distraction and decoys to certain individuals of the pack, some to cut off the escape routes of the prey and finally one or more to finally bring down the prey.

The manipulation game isn't too different from the scenario explained above. When scouting, the idea is not to hide or to skulk in the dark but rather to size up your target emotionally and psychologically. It is the process by which you identify the initial footholds present in their minds and how they could be used to your advantage.

Naturally, when starting the process of manipulation with a stranger, you are usually starting out blind but when you skip the scouting phase altogether, you consign yourself to starting out on the weakest possible footing, further reducing your chances of succeeding.

Watching your target is important

This is the first step and the very foundation of manipulating a target. As shown by the hunting lions, watching or studying gives you a basic info of the target helping you understand the targets habits, likes and dislikes, wants and aspirations of such target that can be exploited. Things that would prove useful in your arsenal for securing the target. A knowledge of the relevant basic info of a target reveals the weak points of such target, providing spots to be exploited to get what is needed and knowing how to trigger such target to get the required result. A good example of those weak points is the human emotions.

As humans, a considerable amount of us tend to act and make decisions under the influence of our emotions and are as a result, slaves to our emotions. Emotions make a man because they are his basest, truest reactions to a situation and most of the time we fall victim to our own emotions, expressing them without control and as such leaving us exposed to the ministrations and knowledgeable tweaking of manipulators. As earlier implied, you must always reserve extreme control over your own emotions and judge every situation logically. This helps you make the right decisions in every situation and also protects you from manipulation as you are the only one with a knowledge of your feelings.

These emotions can act as catalysts to the decision-making process of the human mind without a lot of us realizing it. For example, an altruistic person - that selfless individual who wants to do right by everyone. Such person's need to satisfy everyone can be exploited by the classic guilt trip move, by making them feel sad and unfulfilled and making them do what you want.

The knowledge gleaned from watching a target cannot be underestimated and should be of immense importance to your initial actions concerning such a target, guiding your action and words.

Establishing trust

The importance of trust in manipulation can never be overstated. It is like the key which finally opens a door to a lost store of gems and treasures. just like without the key, you have no access to the treasures which lay inside, so can you not truly manipulate a person without gaining their trust. This is the mistake made by pseudo manipulators and you would do well not to make similar ones. They make the mistake of misjudging how much the target trusts them and as such show their hand too early. As a result, they are exposed to manipulation themselves because they then trust every one of your actions and words to be as a result of their influence.

Trust has always been an active and essential ingredient for a successful human relationship. A child trusts its parent(s) that is why he/she can follow such parent to anywhere without fear for harm. So, it is with is with the targets of manipulation, once you have secured their trust, you become infallible, your decisions are regarded to be the accurate, and your word is held in highest regard.

In some cases, this trust is easily gotten, like in the instance of the altruistic, good-willing and generally naive people. But in other cases, it is not always gotten so easily as one might have to go through various tests to finally earn that trust, but once the trust is finally earned, it is always worth the effort.

You basically have them in the palm of your hand at this level, and they are as clay in the hands of a potter in your own hands - ready to bend to whatever direction you may wish.

The subject of trust is also a critical one as trust is as easy to lose as it is hard to gain. A couple of mistakes could easily cause you to lose the hard-earned trust of a target, and trust when lost, isn't always exactly gotten back. Even if it is gotten back, it is never always in full.

Planning a strategy of approach

Most of the time, for any endeavor to be successful you need a strategy. Referencing the predator/prey scenario earlier stated, a strategy is a means towards an end or ultimate result. The word strategy brings the game of chess to mind. Every smart player knows that to win, a strategy must be in place to achieve such result. If trust is the key to a den of treasures, then your strategy is your plan to avoid the uncanny traps placed around to prevent seekers from reaching the treasure. The manipulation of a target has now become like a game of chess where your every move must be tailored and aimed to getting what you want. It has become a game which for every action of the target, there should be a suitable reaction on the part of the manipulator to help get what is needed.

Since human beings can be quite dissimilar in terms of constitution, intelligence and emotional make-up, it goes without saying that one strategy cannot work for all and different strategies should be employed for different targets and different occasions. One can choose to work a target little by little, slowly but surely getting the required result or one could alternatively leave a "bait" for the target and wait patiently for the bite.

The strategy applied must take into consideration the default emotional state of the target, the level of isolation of the target, the peculiarities of the person as well as the general nature of the person. All of this are very important and neglect of anyone could lead to failure.

Follow only what you see or hear

This is in a way related to the first point. Watching and studying the target would provide you with clues to exploit when working a target. These clues should be your pointers, guiding you on the next step to take or what to say next. But contrary to the first point, this is a warning. You should never try to use a clue or a feeling not present in a particular target against him/her.

As humans, we possess the tendency to judge people based on what we would do in their shoes and not based on what they have shown they would do. You have to kick out this tendency as it could mess with your reactions to the targets actions even without clouding your judgement. It makes you doubt the soundness of your judgement, pushing you to react against what you would do and feel instead of what you can observe the target doing or feeling.

Indiscriminate or excessive use of such could put you in trouble and you could ruin the whole process, causing you to start the whole process all the way from the beginning. Never forget, the idea behind a successful manipulation is determining the targets emotional state and reactions and using this to your advantage. Never let doubt creep in and spoil what is already almost done, only follow what you can see and hear and nothing else.

Conclusion

Understanding the key to manipulation and persuasion is very useful in daily human life. Each facet and form requires its own special skillset to really bring them to life and I hope this audiobook has shown you enough in terms of how to achieve that.

When you understand how to effectively persuade people to your mode of reasoning and manipulate them without their knowledge, you are bound to get more out of situations regardless of whether they are business or relationship scenarios. Eventually, being able to manipulate people to your advantage would increase your influence in life and this influence would bring you success.

Good luck in using the skills you have learned from this book and I hope you experience as much joy in learning as I enjoyed in making this book.

A final word of advice, never give up easily; nothing good ever comes easy and practice makes perfect.

Thank you.

www.ingramcontent.com/pod-product-compliance
Lightning Source LLC
Chambersburg PA
CBHW021128080526
44587CB00012B/1182